BALANCING ACT

BALANCING ACT

Preserving Wealth, Legacy, and Harmony in the Family Business

FRED GUZZI

PAGE TWO
BOOKS

Cataloguing in publication information is available from Library and Archives Canada.
ISBN 978-1-77458-028-8 (paperback)
ISBN 978-1-77458-029-5 (ebook)

Page Two
www.pagetwo.com

Edited by Beth Parker
Copyedited by Crissy Calhoun
Cover and interior design by Setareh Ashrafologhalai

Contents

Introduction

CONGRATULATIONS. You are part of a family business. What began as an entrepreneurial vision has become a much larger enterprise, perhaps still founder-led or now in its second or third generation of leadership. You look around you and see the results of all those years working long nights and weekends when the children were young. Your son, or perhaps your granddaughter, now works in the company. You've watched them grow from someone who used to come in after school to help out into a leader who manages your sales team or runs the family foundation.

Your family's story of hard work and perseverance in your business is an inspiration to Canadians.

As a family business, you are credited with building the economy, providing jobs, creating business opportunities, and contributing to society. Together with the other family-owned businesses in Canada, you employ almost seven million workers every year—that's about thirty-seven percent of the jobs across the country—and you generate over one-third of our gross domestic product.[1]

As well as making a significant contribution to the strength of the North American economy, you make a huge difference to society as a whole. According to a 2017 study, family-run firms contributed fifty-five percent of all charitable donations in North America. That's on top of what you give back to the community in terms of time, resources, and mentorship.

There is a lot of pride in the family brand, especially when you gather to celebrate special events, which could be the launch of a new product or a family member's birthday. You take great pleasure in upholding the family's values and integrating them into the day-to-day work of the company. In return, the community recognizes your company for its leadership. One of your strongest competitive advantages is the trust that your business—as a family-run firm—conjures up in those who buy from you, do business with you, and stay loyal to you.

You have also been able to invest in company activities that are important to the family as well as the business. Like the time when you decided to add a green roof to the warehouse, knowing that the investment would pay for itself over the long term *and* it was the right thing to do. You've made decisions about philanthropy that are personal to you, not just to satisfy a board of investors.

It's been a great ride. So, take a moment to pat yourself on the back.

Now, let's talk about what's keeping you up at night

As you look to the future, what's on your mind? Is it the next sale or who you're going to hire or let go? No. These are issues you've faced many times—you know how to solve them.

What do you really want most for your family and your business?

Successful business-owning families often have a common fear: "How do we keep the vision we originally created for the business? How do we help the next generation create their own vision and keep family harmony along the way?" Their worst fear would be to see the family torn apart because of the business, or the business torn apart because of family conflict.

You are not alone in worrying about these things.

If there is one consistent plea from family-business owners (in most instances, one or both parents), it's for harmony in the family: "I just want everyone to get along." The plea is typically accompanied by the desire to keep the business going no matter what.

Family Enterprise Advisors hear these same concerns over and over again:

- Yes, we want to keep the business going forever, but we also want harmony.
- We want the children to get along now and after we're gone. How do we do that and keep the business healthy?
- The business is everything to us, but the last thing we want in our senior years is to see our family tear itself apart.

The fear is well founded, as the survival rate for family businesses from founding generation to second generation, and beyond, is low. The unfortunate fact is that family businesses do fall apart because of conflict.

Emergence of the family enterprise

No wonder this fear keeps business owners awake at night. When there is strife in the family, the impact is felt far beyond the business aspect of the company. It affects what the financial services industry now refers to as the entire "family enterprise."

The idea of a family enterprise recognizes that what you have as a family-owned company is pretty special. It doesn't end with the business side of the enterprise that makes and/or sells products and/or services. There are many aspects that bring value, such as assets related to real estate, investments, heirlooms, and trusts. Plus, there are assets related to people and relationships, not just money. These include time and resources invested in charitable work and education. And there's everything that makes up the family brand, like the trust the company has built over the years, the entrepreneurial spirit embedded in the family, and the respect earned from the community.

The financial services industry's new understanding of the family enterprise has led to focused interest on keeping them healthy and sustainable. As a result, there are excellent research studies available on the topic in addition to new services that address the challenges faced within a family enterprise. Those in the financial services industry, for instance, are now able to deepen their knowledge and understanding through the program and designation of "Family Enterprise Advisor," offered through the Family Enterprise Exchange (FEX).

Here comes the Family Enterprise Advisor

To better understand the role of a Family Enterprise Advisor, it is helpful to look at how things worked in the past. In general, a financial advisory practice tended to focus on the delivery of services related to investment, financial, and estate planning matters in a business. Issues that came up around family conflict or poor communication were largely ignored. There was even a belief among some business owners (and supported by some advisors) that there were times you simply had to sacrifice family relationships for success in business.

This is no longer the case, at least not with most advisors. Here's a recent example that illustrates what could take place.

Peter came here from Greece when he was a teenager. He got his first job as a pizza delivery boy. Ambitious and anxious to make more money, he traded in his bike for a used van and officially opened his own delivery business. Fifty years later, Peter's trucking company now services all of Ontario and most of western Canada. His wife, Maria, has always worked alongside him, first running the administrative functions and then directing sales.

Now in their late seventies, the couple has set up an appointment with a Senior Wealth Advisor to talk about how best to manage their investments going forward. They also want to review the status of a charitable foundation set up several years ago.

The advisor asks a few questions: "What are your plans going forward in terms of business structure? Are there any changes to know about? Can I assume that your two children, a son and a daughter, are going to be running the business at some point?"

As soon as the last question is asked, the look on both parents' faces changes. The mother throws her hands up in the air and says, "Are you kidding? Neither of them can stand to be in the same room together!" The father doesn't even want to talk about stepping down from his role. The idea that the business may not survive the next phase of ownership is something he's not willing to consider.

In the past, these concerns might have been swept under the table. But not with today's Family Enterprise Services. Maria's reaction is a sign to the advisor that there's conflict going on in the business that could potentially threaten its future. Yes, there is work to be done on the company's investments and charities. But most importantly, someone needs to step in and find a way for the business enterprise—and the family—to move forward cohesively.

Why this book?

This is where I enter the picture.

As a Senior Wealth Advisor at CIBC Wood Gundy, I have spent the past twenty years working with business owners and affluent families. In addition to advising on how to grow financial investments, my work has included various services that complement a successful business and its accumulation of wealth, such as family foundations, charitable organizations, trusts, and succession planning.

During this time, I've seen the need for deeper understanding and support for the family business beyond the nuts and bolts of running a company. This has come directly from my experience working with clients like Peter and Maria who have sat in my office. I have been there when clients reveal that there is serious conflict in the family. I have witnessed breakdowns in communication. I have watched as an underlying family issue or resentment got in the way of a decision about hiring the right CEO or taking advantage of new opportunity.

No one wants conflict in the family or in a business. But harmony doesn't just "happen"; a smooth succession isn't inevitable. Getting along as a family and business go together. And if you ignore one, the other suffers.

When the financial services industry moved toward the development of a more holistic view of the family enterprise, I wanted to formalize the way I'd always approached my clients. In May 2019, I received my certification as a Family Enterprise Advisor. My ongoing study and research in the area of the family enterprise and all it entails continues.

This book is a result of my continued commitment to help the family business—as the family enterprise—and to ensure that the next generation is well prepared and educated on how to keep the enterprise going, and if that's not possible, to at least have the knowledge to make informed decisions about the next right step.

As a family business owner, you have something unique. You owe it to yourself, your family, and all those who benefit from your presence in the world to make sure that your business remains healthy, successful, and focused on the future.

There are going to be some crisis points along the way—I like to call these "lightning bolts." These are the times when a change in business opportunities, or a change in the family, means a change in direction. For example, this could be preparing the next generation to enter the business, or giving a son or daughter who want a way out the options to do so without disrupting what's important for both of you. Like it or not, we're also talking about something unfortunate, like a death in the family, a personal crisis, or a divorce. In 2020, the entire world was impacted by a global pandemic—a huge lightning bolt for every family business.

Lightning bolts threaten harmony. If the family isn't communicating well or getting along before a lightning bolt hits, these are the times when existing cohesion and harmony are most threatened. Managing or overcoming these issues is possible, but only if time has been spent between these lightning bolts to put plans in place for dealing with them.

Your desire as a family business owner or member in a family business "to get along" is not wishful thinking. Seeking family harmony within the business is the first step to moving forward. The research all comes to the same conclusion on this: a focus on family harmony is the right way to go. In fact, a focus on family harmony actually *enhances* success.

Let's look at why the family business is such a unique yet challenging model. There are reasons why conflict may be threatening the business, perhaps even threatening survival. Then we will explore practical steps you can take to build harmony without sacrificing business performance, and how to properly prepare for those inevitable transitions in order to bring success to your family enterprise—in whatever manner you decide to move forward.

FRED

Fred Guzzi, CFA, CFP, CIM, FEA, FMA, FCSI
Senior Wealth Advisor, Senior Portfolio Manager, CIBC Wood Gundy, CIBC Private Wealth

"Some believe you must sacrifice family relationships for success in a family business. But in fact, focus on the family doesn't drain business success—it enhances it."

GLOBAL FAMILY BUSINESS SURVEY OF 2,400 FAMILY BUSINESSES, 2017[2]

PART ONE

THREE CIRCLES OF GOVERNANCE IN THE FAMILY BUSINESS

1

Business Meets Family, Family Meets Business

Overlapping boundaries and uncertain rules that put a business a risk

In this chapter, we'll discuss:

- The three components of a family business: ownership, management, family
- Dynamics that place a family business at risk
- The need for planning "between the lightning bolts"

I WAS SITTING IN a meeting with the father and founder of a successful family business and his son. The son was working in the business, but it was clearly evident—at least to me—that the son felt trapped. He didn't have any interest in the business and didn't want to be a part of it going forward. It was painful to watch. I kept thinking, "You work side by side with your son every day, why can't you see that he's so miserable? Why would you want that for your son? Wouldn't it be better to make a plan for him to get out and finally be happy?"

The father, however, couldn't see it, or wouldn't see it. Even though they'd worked together twenty years, neither of them had ever had an honest conversation about succession. As a result, there was no exit strategy in place, and the father didn't even entertain the thought that the son might not want to keep the business.

Which is exactly what happened. The father died unexpectedly, and almost the next day, the business was sold. The father's vision for the business and how it would last into the next generation was gone. And after two decades of misery, the son was finally free.

No one would wish for the above scenario, but it isn't unique. As we talked about in the introduction, the failure rate of transition in a family business is high: seventy percent[3] by most accounts. The top two reasons are poor communication (sixty percent) and unprepared or reluctant heirs (twenty-five percent). The third relates to lack of shared vision or mission (twelve percent).

These factors certainly apply in the above story. The father and son may have worked side by side, but they clearly were not communicating, at least not about the future of the business. For the father, everything focused on keeping the business going. His vision was not shared by his son. The son lacked passion for the business, even though it had been part of his life since childhood.

The blurred lines between business and family

The above illustrates how dynamics within a family and a business play such a critical role in the success of a family enterprise. You simply cannot separate the two. The business becomes the family, the family becomes part of the business. Family conversations at the dinner table are about the business because the business is an integral part of the family. As a result, children grow up with the expectation that they will start their careers by working at the store or the plant. Or when the matriarch or patriarch makes a final decision about something, it's not because they are the owners or managers, but because they are the parents.

This is very different from a non-family corporation where the distinction between ownership and management are very clear. The separation allows skilled managers to conduct the complicated business of running a large company and owners to objectively evaluate the success of the business, including the work of the CEO and other senior managers. Owners are not expected to be involved in the daily affairs of the company, although they do have the authority to elect directors and are entitled to a share of company profits.

When a family system meets a business system, however, things get complicated. Now there are three components, the third, being that of the family. This creates overlapping boundaries and uncertain rules, depending on where and how family members participate in the business.

The distinctions between the separate components and the assigned roles, responsibilities, and accountabilities are often lost on the players. For instance, in a corporation, the owners would never think of intervening in the affairs of management. In a family-run business, the owner(s) can't help it!

The Three Circle Model of family business

The above challenges have been the subject of study for several decades. In the late 1970s, two professors at the Harvard Business School created the Three Circle Model of family business to illustrate the interaction between the independent and overlapping groups (and interests). The

Three Circle Model is still accepted as the standard model for family businesses, sometimes with slight variations. One, for instance, suggests that the family component is so influential that perhaps its circle should be larger than the other two![4]

The three components (each represented as a circle) are **family, business** (management), and **ownership**. Although each component is considered separate, in a family business, they overlap, with different members occupying one or more circles. Someone who's an owner, for example, occupies all three circles—family, management, and ownership—whereas a family member who works in the business but is not part of the ownership only occupies two.

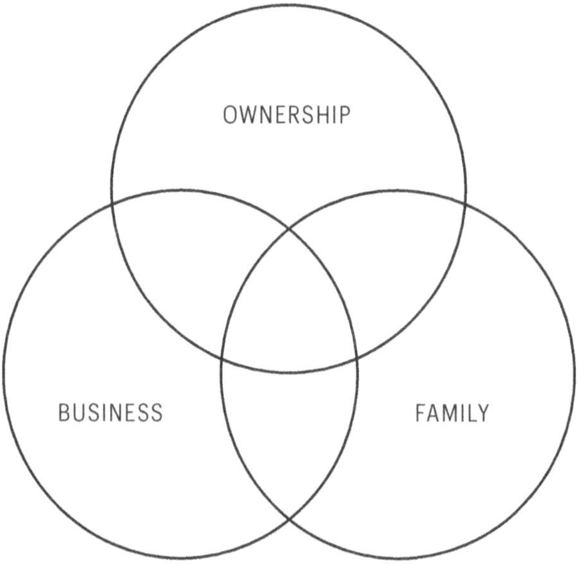

Which segment are you in?

Pause for a moment and ask yourself, "What circle(s) do I occupy in our family business?"

What we can learn from the three circles?

There are a lot of assumptions going on in most family businesses. A father or mother assumes that succession to the next generation is inevitable; a son or daughter assumes they are going to step into a specific role—or not; family members assume they are going to be taken care of equally; non-family members may assume they don't have a voice when it comes to major decisions.

In addition to assumptions, individuals have different perspectives, and therefore different interests, depending on where they sit in the circles. This is particularly the case in the areas where the circles overlap. We noted above the example of an owner interfering with management when there is disagreement on company strategy. Another would be the marriage of a son or daughter. Who has the authority to appoint the new spouse to a decision-making role, such as the board of directors? Or should that even be an option?

The Harvard professors realized this when creating their model and identified seven interest groups:

1. Family members not involved in the business, but who are descendants or spouses/partners of owners
2. Family owners not employed in the business

3. Non-family owners who do not work in the business
4. Non-family owners who work in the business
5. Non-family employees
6. Family members who work in the business but are not owners
7. Family owners who work in the business

When we look at the Three Circle Model, and the various interest groups within the model, it's easy to see why communication, trust, and shared vision are so critical. At various stages and times, ownership, management, and family get mixed together.

Pause again and ask, "Do I recognize the above interest groups in my family business?"

And now the lightning bolts

A business has many moving parts and generally can withstand quite a bit of disruption. But when a family business faces either significant challenges or opportunities, conflicting opinions and reactions across the various interest groups can cause a business to struggle—or fail to reach its potential.

In this book's introduction, we referred to these times as "lightning bolts." Lightning bolts can occur within any of the above three circles.

Family

- Death of a family owner (e.g., father or mother)
- Death of a family member
- Marriage, divorce, or cohabitation agreement
- New blended family

Business

- Bankruptcy or major business failure
- Significant new business opportunity
- Succession
- Regional, national, or global crisis (e.g., a pandemic)

Ownership

- Not having a proper shareholder agreement in place
- Lack of estate planning
- Transfer of shares
- Changes in ownership vision or goals
- Control or trust issues

Lightning bolts are part of the life cycle of a business. You can't avoid them, so you have to prepare for them. These events create a turning point, often unexpected. The turning point could be good or bad, but you can't just sit still and watch. Like a real strike from a lightning bolt, these are the times when a business will be forced to make a decision in one direction or another.

Change can be a real threat to those sitting in any of the seven interest groups identified above. This is magnified when there is existing conflict before the lightning bolt. All of a sudden, the benefits of having a family business, such as being able to work with one another and enjoy greater financial rewards, can quickly become liabilities.

No wonder things get messy

Family members, particularly parents, often turn a blind eye to conflict. The desire for harmony is so great that one or both refuses to see what is happening. In many instances, a parent takes on the burden of being the peacemaker in order to keep things running smoothly—at least on the surface.

The conflict, however, won't magically go away. Operations and management are impacted. As others pick up the slack, there can be growing resentment. Non-family members, caught in the middle of conflict and trust issues, may look for other opportunities.

Functioning in this way is a big risk. This is why many family enterprises bring in expert advisors. It usually takes an outsider to identify the areas of conflict and suggest a new way of effectively managing the family component of the business to move forward.

Sources of conflict include:

- Lack of communication (including family members who literally won't talk to one another)
- Sibling rivalry (talked about or ignored)
- Coalitions between family members (e.g., a brother and sister ganging up on another brother)
- Parents believing they have to take care of everything
- Fear of change (expressed as denial, refusal to try something new, stubbornness, etc.)
- Unresolved issues from childhood (perception of unfair treatment, favouritism, etc.)
- Perceived or real entitlement
- Dependency issues (drugs, alcohol, gambling, etc.)

What other sources of conflict would you add to the list?

Planning for success—however you define it

Even when there isn't serious conflict, a family business needs to put plans in place before a crisis or change in direction forces decisions to be made in one or more of the three circles. We call this planning "in between the lightning bolts." Otherwise, at worst, the business fails to survive, while at best, it stumbles along, moving from crisis to crisis.

Consider a business owner who came for advice because he wanted to retire. Unlike some of his business friends, he just wanted to settle down and relax after all his years of hard work. He figured he'd sell the business, but to his disappointment, no buyer came forward. He had just presumed that someone would come knocking at his door, or one of his two children would want to take over. As it turned out, neither were interested. The owner's lack of planning left him no option but to close down.

There is no right way for a family business to move forward. For many, success means being able to pass the business on to a second or third generation of ownership. For others, it might mean keeping the family enterprise going through foundation work, but closing down the business side of the operation. It also could mean selling a business after retirement and dividing out the proceeds.

None of the above are failures as long as what transpired was part of a plan, with processes and systems to manage the plan and guide good decision-making.

On the surface, this may seem obvious. However, the potential impact that the family component can have on the management and ownership of the family enterprise is too often underestimated, ignored, and/or mismanaged. As a business grows and adds new members over the generations, there are more family members directly involved, interested, or at least connected to the activities of the enterprise. Underlying issues related to lack of trust or feelings of entitlement start to erode its operation.

The proven way to proceed successfully is to separate out the family component first, and then set up the foundational pieces for managing this circle of the enterprise more effectively. From there, best practices can be put in place in order that everyone—individually and collectively—can make more informed decisions about the future, whether it is the next acquisition or a necessary transition.

So, let's get started.

2

Getting Started—The Family Circle

How a family constitution and family values set the foundation for governance

In this chapter, we'll discuss:

- Tough questions and decision-making in the Family Circle
- Connecting family values and family governance
- Giving everyone a voice, if not a vote
- Creating a family constitution tailored to the specific needs of a family

I REMEMBER A PARTICULAR family business where the parents ran the business with their son and two daughters, but it was the father and mother who made the decisions. No one questioned the arrangement, at least not openly, until the mother died and the father remarried. From that point on, the son refused to be in the same room as his dad, even though he held a senior position in the business. The situation was so bad that if he showed up for work in the morning and saw his father's car in the company parking lot, he'd turn around and drive home again.

This was a family that needed to figure out how to make decisions going forward! The new marriage challenged former assumptions around decision-making and in turn impacted how the company did business.

What was good then is no longer good now

Many family businesses don't think about formal governance, particularly if the business is in its first generation of ownership. The owner, typically the patriarch and/or matriarch of a family, makes all the major decisions, perhaps with the counsel of a few trusted advisors. As the second generation becomes more involved in the business, sons, daughters, and even in-laws believe they should have input into how the business operates. By this point, it is likely that there are some who work in the day-to-day management of the company who are not shareholders.

Then one day, someone questions a decision. Or there's a change in circumstances, such as a marriage or a new investment opportunity, and assumptions are challenged:

- Why does Uncle Jim get paid twice as much to do a job that we could hire someone outside the family to do?
- Maria got married last year and her husband wants to work in the business. Do we have to hire him? Does he get paid the same as the rest of us?
- Why does Dad let my brother tell him how to run the business, even though I'm the one who actually works in the business?
- What if some of us want to support a different charity for a change? Or invest in new technology? Or start producing different products?

The informal family system that's been "good enough" up until now is no longer sufficient for dealing with the complexity of owning and running the business. Inevitably, interests overlap between family and business issues (as we saw in the Three Circle Model)—and then conflict arises.

How are decisions made in your family business? Are there assumptions that you question? Have changing circumstances made some decision-making processes problematic?

Introducing family governance

Family governance refers to the rules, processes, and institutions that enable family decision-making and the management of family affairs. Ideally, some kind of formalized governance system is established within the Family Circle *before* conflict. But it is never too late. Today's research continues to show that a well-defined governance structure plays a critical part in the prosperity and longevity of a family enterprise, enhancing both family harmony and family wealth.[5] Without such governance, the chances of a family enterprise making it to the second or third generation fall dramatically.

If the idea of formal governance within the Family Circle sounds too formal or uncomfortable a concept, you are not alone. This is often the reaction when it's first introduced. However, once the concept and the process for creating such governance is explained, most family businesses are open to the idea.

The system—known as the family governance pyramid—has three parts:

- First, there are the **principles** or beliefs unique to each family. These define a family's values and are reflected in the family mission statement. Principles and values don't change because a business takes a new direction or adopts a different structure. Principles endure from generation to generation.
- Second, there are the **policies** that flow out of the principles and values. These cover areas such as how family members treat each other, and they define how decisions are going to be made. Unlike principles, policies can (and should) change as the business and family evolve.
- Third are general **practices**. Practices are pretty straightforward, but unless they are rooted in defined principles and policies, they are likely to be ignored or misused. For example, the practice of holding family meetings will only work if there is commitment to the values of trust and communication to begin with.

The dividing up of family governance into these three Ps (principles, policies, practices) was first introduced by Patricia Angus, an American thought leader in multi-generational family governance and wealth.[6] Angus recognized what she described as a "web of relationships" that exists among family business members and can threaten business survival beyond the first generation of ownership.

Introducing the family constitution

Angus's family governance pyramid is helpful for looking at the essential parts of a family governance system. It shows how the policies (or rules) created by a family business are inexorably linked to family values. This brings us to the idea of a family constitution, sometimes referred to as a family charter.

The use of a family constitution is fairly new; your grandfather may not have heard of the idea! But the concept has been around since the late 1990s. The family constitution sets out a fair process for making joint decisions together as a family and includes policies for the management of family affairs, its businesses, and related entities. What makes a family constitution stand apart from any other agreement is how it's put together. A properly constructed family constitution rests on the family's shared beliefs and values. Once these principles are defined, it's a lot easier to set out the "rules" or policies for governance within the Family Circle in a way that meets its mission and goals.

Give everyone a voice

The most effective way to build a family constitution begins with the most difficult step. You need to get all the players together and enthusiastic about the idea. The message must be clear to everyone: if the family enterprise truly wants to look at opportunities for improvement and sustainability, we need everyone's input. This means we have to get everyone "in the room" (as a group and/or by gathering everyone's input through individual interviews and meetings). This sends a message that those within the Family Circle respect each other's voices, even though everyone may not have a final vote. Note that although face-to-face meetings are ideal, as technology has improved, virtual meetings can be equally effective if it isn't possible to meet in person.

Be clear about attendance. At this stage, cast the net widely so everyone defined as part of the Family Circle feels included. For instance, if there is no clear agreement in the family about including in-laws in decision-making, this needs to be addressed in the constitution. It is best to have full participation in order to demonstrate a commitment to listening to everyone.

Ideally, the owner(s) introduces what's happening in a purpose statement, which could be either in a simple one-page letter or a formal executive summary. The message should state the goal of the process, a timeline, and perhaps some questions to consider ahead of the first meeting.

An example of a purpose statement might be:

As owners [or as founders or family members] we are creating a family constitution to help us grow successfully and to ensure we live in harmony as a family enterprise and preserve our wealth over the generations.

We believe that a family governance system is necessary for both the individuals in our family, the business itself, and our legacy. A constitution, based on our family's mission and values, will give us a fair process for making decisions and serve as a living document for future generations.

Assessments and prep work ahead of time

There are various ways to proceed, depending on the circumstances.

Some families do preparation work ahead of the full meeting, particularly if there are serious conflicts or challenges already at play. It is recommended that the family hire an outside facilitator or process consultant to interview various members of the family as well as non-member senior employees. A neutral party who listens with empathy to concerns, both business and personal, is more likely to uncover issues that family members don't want to talk about with each other. Allowing key family members and senior employees the opportunity to be honest—in a safe environment—is a critical step to improve communication and dynamics.

At the end of this process, an assessment is made, which may or may not be shared with the entire family. The assessment helps identify specific issues that need to be addressed when the family constitution is drafted.

Telling our story

The family then gathers together, ideally in a retreat-like environment where everyone is free from distractions.

The first order of business, however, is *not* to start writing the constitution! Before anyone sets out rules or practices, there needs to be a clear sense of the shared goals and mission of the family. A properly crafted family constitution defines a family as well as that family's values.

The best way to start is through shared stories and family history.

Have you ever gathered with family or with friends and started telling stories? Typically, it begins with "Let me tell you about what happened to me when..." Before long, someone else jumps in with their story, then another, and another. The stories tend to be focused on similar themes—overcoming a challenge, dealing with a difficult person, learning a lesson, reflecting back on a humorous situation.

The same process can be applied at the beginning of the family meeting.

Stories from the founders and all those connected with the business as family members—from teenagers to older adults—remind everyone of their successes, failures, and individual journeys, both good and not so good.

Imagine how the storytelling could take place.

Grandpa tells the story of setting up his first store in the building where he and Grandma lived and raised six daughters. One of the daughters then talks about what it was like living above a noisy store when she was trying to study for her MBA; another recalls the antics she and her siblings got up to during inventory. Someone else tells a story about how their mother would help out local families when they didn't have enough money to pay for groceries. They take a moment to remember the grandmother, who died a few years ago, and how much she wanted them all to get along. A grandson now working at the head office remembers moving into the new office building and the celebration he organized for the staff who moved with them.

The idea behind this exercise is to draw out stories from everyone (not just the ones who like to talk!) and uncover stories not told before. The storytelling doesn't have to be in front of the entire gathering. Some families pair off a grandparent and grandchild, or an uncle and nephew, over lunch to make the exercise more intimate.

As part of this process, many families create a family tree or family schematic that identifies which family members have been involved in the family business and their roles.

Another way to tell stories is to ask about the kind of celebrations and gatherings adopted by the family over the years (sometimes referred to as "rituals"). How do we celebrate as a family? What do we define as a special achievement? A day of rest? These rituals give insight into what needs to be part of future meetings (for example, "We always end the day with a shared meal," or "We always participate in a golf tournament.")

Think about what you might ask about the history of your family business. Who would you ask, and why?

Use the following as a guide.

- Tell us about someone in the family who has been influential in your life and how they've influenced you.
- If you were describing your family to someone else, what would you say?
- What story do you think describes the family best?
- What are you most proud of in the family?

Family stories shape family values and goals

Once stories are shared, the group names the values and goals illustrated by the stories. The exercise starts with a brainstormed list posted where everyone can read it:

- We are a family that perseveres even when times are difficult.
- We have fun together.
- We care about the community around us.
- It's never been solely about financial wealth.
- Harmony is important to us.
- Education has always been our priority.

Each family member is then asked to pick their top five or six values and one or two goals. These again are shared so the group can see which appear the most. If naming values and goals is difficult for some, the following questions may help after listening to the stories:

- What matters most to us as a family and why?
- What impact do we want to have on the world?
- Why do we want to stay together as a family?
- What do we want to be known for?

The following is a sample of a value statement that hangs on the wall of the Henkel Family headquarters in Düsseldorf:

- We put our customers and consumers at the centre of what we do.
- We value, challenge, and reward our people.
- We prioritize activities that result in sustainable financial performance.
- We shape our future with a strong entrepreneurial spirit based on our family business tradition.[7]

Mission statement

Once values and goals are identified, it's time to prepare a short (one to two sentence) family mission statement that answers these questions:

- Who are we?
- What do we stand for?
- What do we want to do?
- How will we get there?

Once the main points are defined, it may be easier to have a smaller group create a first draft, before finalizing the statement.

Here is an example:

Our family mission is to remain a family enterprise over the generations, committed to the well-being of our business, employees, community, and each other, while preserving our wealth and remaining connected to each other.

Family mission statements can be very powerful commitments for moving ahead from one generation to another. Stephen R. Covey, author of *The 7 Habits of Highly Effective People* (1989), also wrote *The 7 Habits of Highly Effective Families* (1997). Covey's statement on the importance of a family constitution still stands today:

By creating and living by a mission statement, families are gradually able to build moral authority in the family itself. In other words, principles get built right into the very structure and culture of the family, and everyone comes to realize that principles are at the center of the family and are the key to keeping the family strong, together, and committed to its destination.

In simple terms these family policies define the "rules of the road" for the family with respect to its relationship to the family business.

How we are going to govern?

Now it's time to focus on what type of policies should be in place as part of the family governance system. Think of this as creating your own rules for how the family component of the business functions. It is important to design an adaptable governance structure where decision-making is perceived to be fair. Systems that work best have two parts: a Family Assembly and a Family Council.

Family Assembly: In setting up any kind of governance structure based on family values, communication and trust must be retained every step of the way. There must be a point where everyone in the Family Circle is given a chance to have their voice heard, which can happen at the Family Assembly. Its purposes are to:

- Provide a forum for the discussion of important family matters
- Reflect together on major decisions or changes in the business
- Elect a smaller group, the Family Council, that meets in the months between the annual assembly

The annual assembly should also set some time aside for activities and storytelling.

Family Council: The Family Council is the executive body or board (not to be confused with a business board). The council answers to the family (not shareholders) and is the voice of the family on behalf of the entire Family Circle. In larger family businesses, there may be a chair and vice-chair, as well as various subcommittees assigned by the council.

In addition to implementing the policies and practices defined in the family constitution, the Family Council has several functions:

- Listen and record input from the full group in order to give everyone a voice (but not necessarily a vote)
- Review the governance system—is it working as planned or are adjustments needed to meet the original objectives?
- Assign tasks to subcommittees or individuals
- Provide updates on work in progress
- Ensure a family meeting for the entire assembly is held annually

Ideally, the council meets quarterly or monthly, depending on its duties. Members are elected by the full assembly and serve a specific term (two or three years). All of this is spelled out in the family constitution.

Some family governance systems add a third group—a **Wisdom Council**—to serve as a sounding board for ideas, mediate conflict, and/or keep the family stories and history alive.

Family subcommittees can vary, depending on circumstances. A family business might always require a standing subcommittee on compensation, for example, but set up a specific subcommittee for an emerging issue, such as estate planning.

It is crucial to establish family meeting rules or guidelines and have them agreed to by the participants either before the first meeting or at the first meeting. Include who chairs the meeting, who implements decisions made, how disagreements are handled, what the expectations for attendance and participation are, how individuals are expected to treat each other, and so on. For an example of a meeting agenda and family rules, see chapter six.

Other tips for creating a family constitution

Facilitation: An outside facilitator for at least part of the meeting encourages everyone to participate and monitors what's happening in the room. This role could be filled by a Family Enterprise Advisor.

Fun time: There should be time set aside for activities that are not work-related, such as sports, games, movie night, etc. Remember that one of the reasons for the meeting is to build trust and communication.

Transparency: Provide a timeline for the meeting, and explain what will happen afterward so everyone knows what to expect.

Facility: Meet somewhere that is comfortable and accessible for everyone. Families often choose a cottage, retreat centre, favourite golf course, etc.

Customization: The family mission and values, along with its governance system, form the core part of a family constitution. But include other elements to make the family constitution work for your own family. It can include:

- Family definition: Who are we talking about? (e.g., "all the descendants of…")
- A glossary of terms to ensure everyone understands the language in the constitution

The final step: ratification

Once all the elements of a constitution are discussed at a full Family Assembly, and/or gathered from interviews, an assigned working group drafts the document. During this time, the working group may go back to different family members to ask specific questions or test out ideas. The family constitution is then presented to the entire group, and a vote taken to approve it. Ideally, this is done at an event with everyone present. The vote could, for example, be held on the first official meeting of the new Family Assembly.

The constitution is a living document

Remember:

- There is no one way to develop a family constitution. Each constitution is unique.
- It could be two pages or fifty, depending on the complexity of the business and size of the family.
- It is a living document that should evolve over time, with procedures in place for this evolution to take place.

The above points are worth emphasizing, particularly when introducing your new constitution. It assures members that what they have created is not cast in stone but is designed to be adjusted as circumstances change.

It's worth doing!

Governance is going to be required in all three circles, but the starting point has to be the Family Circle. This is the hardest—and the most critical. Businesses that embody their values in everyday practices and routines get better results.

Why begin with the most difficult? We start there because this is the best way to build the trust and communication needed to govern the business wisely. Without open, honest communication, and a trusted environment to share such communication, it's going to be extremely difficult to navigate those lightning bolts.

Creating your family constitution is one of the most worthwhile steps you can take. Your own customized governance system, tailored to the context of your family and its values, is a "secret sauce" proven to give tremendous competitive advantages. By embedding your values into everyday practices and routines, your family is going to enjoy a higher level of communication and trust, prepare the next generation in a way that is helpful and empowering, and share a sense of vision beyond what you do each day—all the factors missing in family businesses that falter.

In the words of Dr. Justin Craig, professor of family enterprise at the Kellogg School of Management:

The [family enterprises] that get it right start with understanding the value of values. They get that this is what distinguishes them in the market. It's their DNA, *their secret sauce.*[8]

3

The Business Evolves—The Owners' Council

Ownership as moral obligation, not just a right

In this chapter, we'll discuss:

- Evolution in ownership and types of ownership
- Role of an Owners' Council
- Questions that lead to policies
- Rights and obligations of owners
- Preparing the next generation of owners

THE IRVING EMPIRE is a classic family business story. In 1882, grandfather J.D. Irving opened a sawmill and general store in Bouctouche, New Brunswick. The business was small, but his son, Kenneth Colin (K.C.), possessed the drive and talent to grow the company far beyond his father's wildest dreams. Under K.C.'s leadership, the family business was transformed into a multi-billion-dollar conglomerate that included manufacturing, lumber, oil, shipbuilding, construction, and trucking businesses, among others.

K.C.'s three sons, James, Arthur, and Jack, entered the business at an early age—also typical of a family business. After K.C. died, ownership and operation of the company was divided between the sons and their respective children. James got forestry and shipbuilding; Arthur, energy; and Jack, real estate and construction.

While their father was alive, things ran fairly smoothly. Harmony and unity were part of the Irving brand; whatever the differences were between the brothers stayed mostly invisible to the outside observer. But as the third and then fourth generations moved into various management and ownership roles within the company, the clashes between interests and personalities heightened.

Piece by piece, the harmony and unity prized by K.C. began to fall away. The *Wall Street Journal* quoted one of the grandsons, Kenneth Irving, as saying "balancing 'cousin to cousin, uncle to uncle' relationships in a business environment was 'complex.'"[9]

The problems were more than complex; they were messy. One of the brothers had to fire his own son, and there were court challenges over the terms of a family trust because of a strongly held belief by at least one family member that not everyone named in the trust had contributed equally to the business.

Kenneth eventually left the business altogether. According to the *Wall Street Journal* piece, it got to the point that he and his brother (the two remaining grandsons) rarely talked to each other. The Arthur Irving Family Trust eventually bought out the rest of the shares. Today, Irving Oil and the Irving family enterprise is still considered one of the most successful in Canadian history. The unfolding story is also an example of the dynamics at work in a family business as it grows and expands into third and fourth generation of ownership.

"The whole Irving story has exploded," observed business writer Gordon Pitts, who has written extensively about family-owned empires. "As cousins entered, it [got] much more difficult."[10]

Three stages of ownership

There is no predicting the manner in which ownership might evolve in any one business. As time passes, and the business and the family grows and changes, issues around ownership are going to get increasingly complex. Just as in any business relationship, once there is more than one individual invested in the enterprise, there needs to be agreement and communication about how the individuals behave as owners.

There is also a stage where it becomes critical to distinguish between the roles of ownership and management. It is common for founders themselves to not realize the difference between an owner's role and management's role because they have been doing both. This stage inevitably comes when a company incorporates and formalizes the titles and responsibilities related to the roles of directors, shareholders, and officers.

All of the above applies to an expanding family business. But what is unique about family-owned operations is the inherent complexity of family dynamics that intensify as the ownership life cycle unfolds. Once ownership and/or management are expanded to children, siblings, cousins, or even non-family members, ownership becomes a mix of interests, commitment, and entitlement. In short, the family interferes.

Those who study family business identify three stages of ownership in a family business. Throughout these stages, business relationships are coloured by family relationships.

1. In the beginning, there is the **owner-managed business** in which ownership of the company is in the hands of one person.
2. At the next stage, **sibling partnerships**, the ownership is divided more or less equally among a group of siblings, some or all of whom work in the business.
3. By the third and fourth generation, ownership is described as cousin companies or **cousin consortiums**. Ownership is spread across a group of owners (and most do not take part in the day-to-day management of the business). All the family dynamics we talked about in chapter one are now at play (in-laws, divorces, remarriage, etc.) and all parties have varying degrees of interest, commitment, and competency.

Given what we know about these three stages, advisors who work with family businesses recommend that the enterprise set up an Owners' Council. An ownership structure will already be in place, perhaps divided between two parents. But down the road, as ownership begins to divide into multiple family members and possibly non-family owners, an Owners' Council is critical for the long-term stewardship of the enterprise.

An Owners' Council is not a legal entity, but like the Family Council, it provides a forum for ownership concerns that might otherwise be avoided because they represent difficult conversations and potential family conflict.

If the ownership group is large at this point, it is wise to elect a representative group of owners to the council. In a corporate structure, ownership reports to an annual shareholders' meeting. In a family business, the owners, as the Owners' Council, report to the annual Family Assembly.

Role of the Owners' Council

One of the most important roles for the Owners' Council is to articulate the vision and goals for the company (stated in the family constitution). It then addresses the ways in which to execute them. This becomes the company's strategic direction. Once determined, it should be relayed to the company board of directors to implement.

The vision encompasses three aspects:

- Growth and profitability targets, distribution targets, etc.
- Desired values regarding how the business operates
- Succession objectives

Without a vision that's clearly communicated to management and the family, somewhere down the line there are going to be trust issues, control issues, intergenerational dynamics issues—all the factors that arise when there are assumptions but no stated overall strategy.

The Owners' Council also manages those difficult issues in a family business where there is overlap between, or even misunderstanding of, the roles of ownership and management. In the governance structure of *any* business, ownership must guide the board in how the business is governed. Questions to be solved include how to evaluate risk, what investments and strategies are in keeping with owners' interests, or what share structure should be in place.

The above can become extremely difficult in a family business. Family members might raise concerns like, "Why does my brother draw the same share in the business that I do, even though he's never around?" or "I'm the founding owner. Why shouldn't I have the final say in every decision?"

There's an additional complexity when individuals may be equals as members of a family, but they are not necessarily equals as owners in the business. The Owners' Council needs to weigh any decisions against the six kinds of ownership in the family business and their differing levels of interest and motivation.

As you read the list, ask yourself, "What kind of owner am I and what does this mean to me and to the business?"

1 An operating owner with direct responsibility for running the business

2 A governing owner who is a full-time overseer but not involved in the daily management of the family business, such as a chairman of the board of directors

3. An involved owner who is not employed in the business but takes a genuine interest in the company, offering support to management as appropriate

4. A passive owner who collects dividends but abdicates responsibility for the business to others and makes no conscious decision to stay actively engaged

5. An investor owner who is similar to a passive owner except if they are dissatisfied with their returns, they may decide to keep or sell their ownership

6. An owner who is not engaged in the business or especially knowledgeable about it but nonetheless is proud to be an owner

Questions for the Owners' Council

The Owners' Council provides a forum where questions can be discussed rationally, with minimal emotion, with both family and business interests kept in mind. Once everyone's voice is heard, the council can strike some kind of agreement as to the interaction between owners and management, including the board of directors, owners, and the family.

Below are some specific situations, which need to be worked out ahead of the question being asked. Every council will design its own policies—in consultation with the family and management—for wise decision-making.

SPECIFIC QUESTION OR NEED	POLICIES TO BE DETERMINED
A sibling announces, "I want out of the company ownership, and I want to collect my share. How much do I get?" The founder, the father or mother, dies unexpectantly, and everyone asks, "Now what happens to their shares?" Do they automatically transfer to the eldest child? Is the family okay with this expectation? Is the eldest child okay with it? What about the younger brother or sister? What happens if the surviving parent remarries? Does the new spouse have ownership? One of the owners asks that her shares be transferred to her own son or be divided with her new husband. Is everyone okay with this, or should there be restrictions on the transfer of shares?	How and when can ownership interests be sold or transferred? When the family is going through a major transition with a sibling getting married (or divorced!), for example? Is it time to revisit the share structure? How are decisions made? Who can own shares and who can vote on them? Who can appoint directors? What are the rules around confidentiality and conflicts of interest?
The founder wants to give a long-standing employee who is not a family member a share in the business in order to reward her and secure her commitment.	Can non-family members be owners? Does the business welcome non-family members as employees or rely on non-family management or both? Can non-family members be appointed to the board of directors?
There is a disability, retirement, bankruptcy, divorce, or an unresolved dispute between business owners and shareholders that raises the question, "How do we divide up ownership fairly, if not equally?"	Does a buy-sell agreement need to be put in place?
Are the owners looking for growth or harvest? That is, are the owners looking for rapid growth or growth at a steadier pace? Younger owners are typically more willing to invest for long-term gains; those who've worked hard in the company for many years may want to finally enjoy the fruits of the labour.	What risks is the owner willing to take? What strategy presents the most or least risk? What level of risk is best for the business and the family? What level of profitability is desirable? What level is acceptable? What is unacceptable?
Do the owners want a diversified multi-business company, or do they want to stay in one industry? Do they want to be local, regional, or global?	Revisit the vision for the company. What is the long-term goal? What are the values we want to preserve?

Buy-sell agreements

Inevitably, ownership in the business is going to change. Someone will want to pull out as an owner, expand their options, or there will be some kind of decision-making impasse. The remaining owners then have to decide how the business continues. The Owners' Council can help guide the family through the setting up of a buy-sell agreement.

When the change is the result of a death, there are four options to consider:

1. Close down the business (though after all the time, energy, and money invested, this may not be a practical option)
2. Continue the business with a new partner (e.g., the spouse of the deceased)
3. Sell the shares (Who will buy them and at what price?)
4. Purchase the shares from the deceased owner's estate

The Owners' Council may choose to put a buy-sell agreement in place in anticipation of the above. A buy-sell agreement states 1) the "triggering events," 2) the value of the business (or a calculation method), 3) how it is funded, and 4) how the purchase will occur if a partner has a triggering event.

It's critical to have funding for the share purchase in place; without it, the remaining owners may not be able to afford to buy the shares or they may have to compromise the business's finances to do so. For succession planning, life insurance is the best way to fund a buy-sell agreement. Upon execution of a buy-sell agreement, each partner takes out a life insurance policy equal to the value of their ownership interest. A financial or insurance advisor can advise on how to set one up.

Consider this scenario if you don't have a buy-sell agreement in place: you and your business partner may work great together, but if your partner passes away, would you and your partner's spouse be as compatible?

Preparing owners to be owners: rights vs. obligations

One of the most important obligations of the Owners' Council is to ensure future owners—the ensuing generation—are equipped to be wise, thoughtful, and intelligent in their roles. On the surface, it seems simple. A family member owns shares in the company by right with no special training or certification required. But the role of an owner who guides the company and interacts with its board, managers, and the family can have a huge impact on the business's ultimate performance.

Those born into a family business grow up with different competencies and ambitions. One daughter may grow up in the business, with the knowledge and commitment to effectively lead it and decide what's best for the firm and the family. A younger son may grow up enjoying his allowance and spending most of his time as far away from the business as possible. Both have the "right" of ownership, but only one understands the obligations.

Ownership implies careful stewardship. The Owners' Council can reinforce the message to current and future owners that those who accept ownership in a family business have a moral obligation and responsibility to the family, the business, and the community around them.

Just what do good owners do in a family business?

While owners have certain legal rights and powers, what distinguishes outstanding owners in a family business is their willingness to do what's right in the long run for other shareholders, the business itself, the family, employees, and the wider community.

When owners clearly understand their roles and have been properly prepared for ownership, they make it possible for managers to do their jobs in an optimal way. When owners look for processes and ways to keep communication open and give everyone a voice, they gain the trust of the family.

> The following is a good reminder to all owners: ownership, as a legal matter, is a bundle of rights and obligations. In a family business, ownership is also a moral matter.

We return for a moment to the story about the Irving family. Joan Irving, wife of grandson Arthur, was also caught up in the contentious ownership and subsequent succession issues that engulfed the Irving dynasty. In a 2012 interview, Joan's comment said it all: "This terrible business of succession seems to have devastating effects."[11]

Ownership questions don't have to end up with devastating effects. Good governance is about good decision-making and communication. With a clear understanding of the role of owner and an Owners' Council in place, family enterprises are much more likely to weather the challenges that come with second and third generation ownership—and meet the challenges in the Business Circle, which we'll explore in the next chapter.

4

The Enterprise Prospers—The Business Circle

Growing a business while navigating the tricky waters of family dynamics

In this chapter, we'll discuss:

- Balancing the priorities and needs of the business with participating family members
- Business structures as the family enterprise grows and evolves
- Values and skills of an effective board member
- Solving performance management and HR issues

REMEMBER HOW the circles overlapped in the Three Circle Model? The priority in the Business Circle is overall performance.

The Business (or Management) Circle of the family business is focused on making sure the business reaches its full potential. Unlike non-family businesses, however, in a family-run enterprise, family members are involved on the management side and in leadership roles. As we know, family members bring with them differing motivations, interests, expectations, and abilities. When performance overlaps with the family members' need for inclusion or reward, the health of the entire enterprise is at stake.

In the movie franchise The Godfather, the youngest of three sons is chosen instead of the older brother to be the successor of the New York Mafia family business. Frederico Corleone, known as Fredo, is notorious for his shortcomings—incompetence, bad business ideas, and heavy drinking, among others. At one point, the family business tries moving him to Las Vegas to keep him out of trouble. Fredo's mess-ups and immaturity become a dangerous liability to the business, eventually leading to tragic consequences (particularly for the hapless Fredo).

The situation of having a Fredo in a family business strikes an unfortunate chord with those who've experienced first-hand what happens when a family member wants to be an employee in a family business but lacks the skill or aptitude for the job. Known as the "Fredo factor" or "Fredo effect," this kind of nepotism has a toxic impact on a business, threatening good management and performance.

Unfortunately, the Fredo effect does not happen just in Hollywood. A study by *Family Business* revealed that approximately one-third of family businesses admit to having an employee who is an impediment to the business and only has a job because they are family.[12]

The growth and sustainability of the Business Circle depends on a fine balance between the needs of the business and the expectations of family members. In order to keep this balance, Family Enterprise Advisors recommend specific business structures and rules to clarify roles and ensure good decision-making, transparency, and clear communication.

The benefits are both immediate (with decision-making processes in place for day-to-day operations) and long term (positively affecting continuity, transition, and succession planning).

The areas to be addressed in this section are:

- Formalization of governance structures within the business itself, i.e., the management team, advisory board, and board of directors

- Policies and management plans around performance and human resources, in particular for the planning and development of key managerial roles
- Succession planning well in advance of any transition

Formalization of business structures

At some point during the first or second generation of ownership, the owners realize that they can't "do it all." In order to grow, specific skills—skills that family members may not have!—need to be added in marketing, sales, finance, human resources, and so on.

The resulting management team now has the responsibility for operations and profitability. They are the ones with first-hand insight into what is happening on the ground (unlike, for instance, a passive or proud owner). As senior leadership, they also are able to step back, see the bigger picture, and assess whether or not the business is going to achieve its potential.

Setting up a board of directors is another step in the creation of more formalized structures.

Most owner-operated businesses start out with some form of advisory group. Made up of one or more trusted friends and/or family members, the group functions as a rubber stamp for the owner's decisions. The advisory board is an interim solution between a fully family-run board and a board of directors with one or more formally appointed non-executive outside director.

The legal responsibilities of a board member in a family business and those on the management team are no different than in a non-family business.

- The management team is accountable to the board of directors for results. Management and the board are accountable to the owners and/or shareholders for the overall performance of the enterprise.
- Members of a board are required to keep themselves informed as to what the corporation is up to and on matters relevant to the enterprise of the corporation generally. The board may—and typically will—exercise its authority through the actions of the senior management when appointing and evaluating leadership (e.g., the CEO, CFO, and senior managers).
- The board's responsibility—and the liability that comes with it—can't be abdicated or delegated. Whether the issue on the table is buying another business or investing in new technology, the judgment that each board member is expected to exercise in the conduct of their role is their own. In the case of a corporate decision that turns out to be the wrong one, it is no good for a board member to claim that the decision was made at the insistence of a particularly aggressive shareholder (who happens to be his brother).

The above may be clearly understood in the case of a publicly owned business, but is often overlooked in the case of a family business. Family business boards must act on behalf of stakeholders with multiple and potentially conflicting agendas and still keep their objectivity. A father (and owner) may want to fire the CEO who happens to be his son-in-law, but he doesn't want to create a rift between him and his daughter. Or he wants to help out an unemployed, unskilled nephew by making him marketing director, but his talented CEO threatens to quit if he does so.

Values and roles for board members in a family business

There are many resources that detail the roles and responsibilities of senior management (officers) and directors. In this chapter, we want to highlight the role they play in a family business in ensuring family conflicts and the financial or career interests of family members don't endanger the long-term profitability of the company.

In executing this role, it is advised that an effective director demonstrates the following when dealing with the family, the owners, management, and other board members:

Trust: Different family members with different interests perceive things differently. Effective directors have to find ways to develop trust with family and non-family leadership and management. In every action, they must be constantly aware of tensions created over perceived injustices. One way to do so is to build relationships with new family members who are added to the board, establishing trust right from the beginning. Another is to take the time needed to meet with the Family and Owners' Councils to share information and provide updates.

Objectivity: Whether or not they are outsiders to the family, board members should be chosen for their objectivity. For example, in the early stage of a family business, founders and family members may view company assets as belonging to them. Directors should be able to challenge these assumptions without emotion and offer wise counsel on how the assets and profits of the business are best distributed or reinvested for the good of the whole.

Objectivity is also established from the beginning by making sure that the board isn't packed with golfing buddies or made up entirely of family members. If something goes wrong in a company—especially if it involves a family member—a manager is going to find it easier to report concerns to a director who is outside of the family.

Fairness and transparency: Family business is all about communication: everyone needs to feel that they have a voice, if not a vote. Board members need to make sure that the process for making major decisions (such as buying a new business or expanding into new markets) is transparent and aligns with the overall mission set by the family.

Fairness and transparency are particularly important when it comes to human resources. Directors have to be willing to work with management on bonus plans and merit-based guidelines for hiring and promoting, with input from the owners based on the overall strategic plan and goals for the business.

Listening and questioning: Families don't speak with one voice (even if that's the intent of the owner!). Board members have to be willing to listen to multiple points of view and engage in difficult conversations to find out what's really going on. Asking well-informed, thoughtful questions creates an environment that encourages candid discussions and healthy debate, instead of emotional reactions.

By taking time to understand the family's goals, relationships, and fears, an effective director is able to present issues in a thoughtful way. One US board talked about sending a director to the annual Family Council meeting to find out "the sacred cows." By doing so, the board was able to avoid a potential conflict when setting priorities.

Ability to mediate family influence: The ability to mediate without alienating is critical on a family board. If a manger isn't showing up for work, and that manager is the owner's brother—the board and senior management must step in to make a decision. Or if the business requires investment to reach its full potential but the owners are taking out every cent, someone has to present the case to the owners without alienating the family. These conversations need to take place in order to keep the business performing at its best. This won't happen if a talented CEO quits in frustration, or resources aren't appropriately reinvested back into the business.

Patience: The input of boards and advisory councils is sometimes unwelcome. This is especially apparent when succession is discussed. Directors in a family business can introduce the benefits of planning well in advance, initially introducing the topic at the Family Assembly so the process is seen as open and transparent. The board then needs to work with the Family and Owners' Councils in developing that plan.

Mentorship: Directors can play an important role in preparing family members who have joined the business and may aspire to run it one day. Outside directors typically come from industry and bring valuable outside experience. Directors who are family member can do the same, in addition to passing on stories of the family history and lessons learned along the way.

Can I really fire my father?

Performance and career management of both family and non-family employees can become fraught with emotion in a family business. Understandably, a father may not want to deal with difficult questions, such as "Why does your son get paid twice what he'd earn as director of marketing in any other company?" The situation can be even worse than that. What if the question becomes "Why can't we just fire him and put someone in place who is actually going to help the business increase sales?"

It's up to those doing the hiring—the managers and the board—to keep the business healthy. This is best done through merit-based policies and processes for human resources designed to reduce the potential for favouritism of family employees and to encourage the promotion of the most qualified candidate. Hiring practices should be accompanied by formal job descriptions that define roles and expectations and set out the process for performance reviews.

The same applies for succession planning, discussed in detail in the next chapter. A son or a sister may have all the right intuition, work ethic, and leadership traits to be successful, but this doesn't mean they know how to run a business.

Review the list below and ask yourself, "Have we answered these for our business? What are the consequences of not answering them?

What can we put into place so there are no misunderstandings?

What is needed to practice good stewardship and move the business forward?"

- Do non-family members have access to management positions?
- Are we going to use compensation benchmarking to set salary ranges for all employees (family and non-family alike)? If not, what system will we use that is viewed as fair by the family and prudent to the business?

- What process do we want to put in place to groom successors for senior roles? Is this process only open to family members? What happens if no one fits the qualifications we require?
- How are we going to determine bonus packages and payments?
- What process will prevent nepotism and promote the most qualified candidate? (Even if this means promoting a younger sister over an older brother.)
- Is the next generation ready to assume high-level or full management responsibility in the business? If not, what needs to be done to change the situation?

The recommended way to keep the business component of the family enterprise running smoothly is to see the Business Circle as a place that keeps the business healthy with structures and policies to help neutralize emotional decisions, while the Family Circle deals with family issues.

Now that we've looked at the family business through the lens of the Three Circle Model, we return to two of the most difficult processes that family businesses face: business transitions and succession. This is where the structures and policies we've created prove valuable for balancing emotions and leading to well-thought-out decisions.

PART TWO

RESOURCES AND SKILLS FOR SUCCESSION PLANNING AND DECISION-MAKING

5

The Human Side of Succession Planning

Creating good endings and new beginnings

In this chapter, we'll discuss:

- The difficult topic of "stepping back"
- A succession planning process
- Meeting tips and setting guiding principles
- Bringing about a good ending

"A benefit of surprises is that they're often a prod to action . . . Some surprises help people see that the status quo needs to change. Some surprises underscore that transformation is happening already."

BILL AND MELINDA GATES 2019 annual letter[13]

WE'VE TALKED about the unexpected lightning bolts in a family-owned business that result in an inevitable transition. But not every lightning bolt is a surprise. One major transition that hits absolutely every family business at some point is a change in ownership—and typically a subsequent change in company management. Unlike a real lightning bolt, it is possible to prepare for this kind of major transition. Unfortunately, most family businesses don't.

According to a 2019 survey by PricewaterhouseCoopers, forty-eight percent of family business owners plan to pass ownership and/or management of their business to the next generation, but forty-seven percent of them don't have a succession plan, and twenty-seven percent haven't involved the next generation in preparing for the changes.[14]

It's as if the owners think they are going to livc forever.

The legal, tax, and estate planning side of the matter

Family business succession is the process of transitioning the management and the ownership of the business to the next generation of family members. The transition likely includes family assets as part of the process.

Family Enterprise Advisors are typically drawn into the succession process when there's a need to look at issues related to technical aspects, such as legal, financial, tax, and estate planning. However, it's the family that ultimately determines if succession works or not. Before any of these measures are implemented, let alone planned for, the family should have a succession process in place that transitions not just the business and the estate effectively but also manages the family's and owner(s)' expectations through the process.

All too often, this is not the case. For example, consider what happens in a scenario where an owner is confident there are no successors in the family with the ability to take over the business. When setting up the tax and legal side of the family business succession plan, he instructs an advisory firm to arrange for the sale of the business to a senior employee.

The owner's failure to share his intentions clearly with the family causes conflict even if it is a wise decision. The employee may have been the best thing for the business in terms of leadership and future growth, but without the support of the family in the decision, there are signs of trouble even before the new owner steps into his role.

Successful succession plans must balance the needs and goals of the family, as well as the needs and goals of the business. As discussed in the first four chapters, family members—to varying degrees—are part of the management and ownership of the company. This complicates matters. All three circles of interest and the accompanying dynamics will be part of succession planning, whether there's a plan in place or not. While financial and legal advisors are assessing potential risks to the business, emotions are going to arise on the family side.

Dealing with these emotions and defusing potential conflict can only happen when the family is integrated into the process. It is therefore critical that succession is talked about before any decisions are made—and certainly well before the passing of the owner.

Talking (or not talking about) succession

Ironically, bringing up the subject is often the most difficult task.

Owners, typically a parent, are notoriously reluctant to talk about succession, let alone retirement or any suggestion that they might step back from their responsibilities. Some expect a difficult process and so, for the sake of family harmony, deliberately avoid talking about it. Others have their mind made up—"Of course, the business is going to my eldest child"—even if it's just an assumption on their part.

The topic needs to be introduced and followed up with open and constructive conversation about the overall vision for the family business. This isn't going to happen at a single meeting. The process takes time and needs to be expanded beyond one or a select few individuals.

> Ask yourself, "Is the current generation (or one senior member) ready to let go of responsibility for the direction and control over the family business?"

There's no better place for these kinds of discussions than the dedicated communication forum discussed in chapter two, the Family Assembly, as well as in ongoing Family Council and Owners' Council meetings. Some may even choose to call a family meeting specifically for the topic or to set up a succession subcommittee of the Family Council. Succession planning can tackle both the topics of management and ownership, or deal with one at a time. If this is the case, the management succession process should be carried out first so that the ownership succession plan reflects and supports what's decided.

There are going to be some tough decisions to make before planning begins. Ideally, your family constitution has already defined who participates in open discussion, who has a vote, and who makes the final decisions. With agreed-upon principles already in place, conversations can be driven by what's best for the whole, rather than a free-wheeling forum driven by self-interests, fears, and assumptions. If such guidelines and rules are not in place, these issues need to be talked about and defined before any discussion takes place around succession. (See chapter six.)

Consider the suggested planning process below and how it can work in the family and in the ownership circles. No two family enterprises are the same. Your plan has to address your unique situation. As we've emphasized throughout this book, regardless of who makes the final decision (and it could be solely the owner), it is critical that those with an interest as family members have a chance to have their voices heard.

Suggested succession planning process

1. Clarify the family vision

Ideally, the family vision is already in place before succession planning begins. At a full family meeting, such as the annual Family Assembly, revisit the family mission statement, goals, and values to begin an open discussion.

Listen to the individual visions of family members and address the following questions:

- Who is interested in working in the business? Who would prefer a different path?
- Is there a logical successor in the management of the business?
- Does the successor have to be a family member?

2. Establish the owner's vision

The owner's vision can be established in various forums such as in a family meeting, with the Family or Owners' Council, through individual interviews between the owner and key senior staff, with a succession subcommittee, or with financial planning advisors. Advisors are particularly helpful in ensuring the estate is sufficiently diversified so that the owner's children who are not active in the business can be treated fairly alongside those receiving an interest in the business.

Consider the following questions:

- How does the family vision align with the owner's plans for the business?
- Does the vision include keeping the business in the family?
- Is the owner willing to consider transferring ownership of the business during their lifetime? If so, when will they be ready to let go?
- Who among your family members or employees has the qualifications to lead the business? If no one comes to mind, who might you groom to take over?
- What does the owner view as their ideal role once succession is complete? (i.e., What do you want to do with the "rest of your life"?)

3. Set the ground rules

Ideally, these have already been defined in the family constitution. Review the rules for how to communicate in a meeting.

4. Specify guiding principles and objectives

Guidelines, prepared in a family meeting, are finalized for the succession process by a smaller representative group (Family Council, Owners' Council, or succession planning subcommittee). Determine the guiding principles for business succession and asset transfers. These should align with the family goals and mission statement (see example below).

5. Explore all options and possible strategies

The succession planning subcommittee now develops transition options to present to the Family Assembly. Family members have the opportunity to discuss these options at a full family meeting. This ensures that everyone clearly understands what is being communicated and each option's potential impacts. Discuss what-if scenarios and implications of agreements. Refine where necessary. Agree on the best option and formulate a plan to get there.

6. Complete structures and agreements

The succession (business) plan is presented, revised, and approved by the current and future owners.

7. Determine timeframes

The current and future owners, along with the planning subcommittee, set a timeframe that addresses when the transition will take place. Be clear about who the new owner(s) will be, and recommend ways to ease the transition.

8. Prepare successors

The current and future owners and the planning subcommittee may want to include members of the advisory board or board of directors in the process of preparing the successor. Consider:

- How are we going to prepare the successor (ownership and management)?
- What do they need (individual plans for each)?
- Who is going to do this?

9. Communicate to family

It's vital to communicate at each phase along the way. Use family meetings to update on progress, review the timeline, gather ongoing feedback, and make informed decisions, so that (at least) the majority of the family feels comfortable with the overall process and plan. Communicate the final decision along with the preparation plan. The final succession plan shouldn't be a surprise!

Meeting and process tips

- Keep discussions at full family meetings focused on bigger picture issues, e.g., the overall vision, the owner's vision, values as established through family history, and what's best for the business.
- Remind everyone that no decisions are being made at these full family gatherings. The purposes are to inform, educate, and obtain feedback.
- Consider using an outside facilitator so everyone can participate and the discussion follows the agreed-upon rules and guidelines. An outside facilitator assures members that the process is being guided objectively by someone without a personal interest in the final result.
- Transparency and patience are critical. Remind those who believe they have all the answers to let others talk. It is through the honest declaration of future ownership intentions that the family can move forward into the future with a plan to protect their wealth and retain family harmony.
- Consult chapter seven on emotional intelligence for skills helpful in navigating emotional issues.

Guiding principles and objectives

Succession guiding principles highlight the main interests of the family and state preferences for how a plan is put together. It's best to outline these at a full family meeting. Succession objectives are similar in concept but include specific outcomes (e.g., fifty percent ownership, ten percent shares). Guidelines keep the discussion at the big-picture level.

What are your guiding principles for succession planning? Check the list below to see what others have used.

Here's a typical set of guiding principles:

- Family harmony is to be preserved.
- Parents are assured of a secure income for the rest of their lives.
- Adult children are assured of a secure income as long as they participate at a certain level in the business.
- A viable business is maintained.
- There will be fair distribution of assets in the estate plan.

It may not be feasible to meet all the guiding principles. If this is the case, ask the family to prioritize their guiding principles to find out which ones are not negotiable.

A word on "grooming" the next generation

One of the most important parts of any successful succession plan is the preparation of those stepping into new roles.

Existing owners may not believe that a son or daughter, or even a star employee, is ever completely ready for the role. However, knowing that their successor has been prepared well ahead of time by someone trusted to do the job provides some level of comfort. The same applies to misgivings by other family members, who have their own perceptions of their siblings, nephews, or cousins.

Successors need to learn the management tasks, and those watching over them need to evaluate how well they do. This is necessary both to satisfy the family that decisions are being made fairly and to protect the viability of the business. For example, one family put a young adult on the company board of directors, with non-voting shares, with the promise that once she proved her ability on the board, she could then buy the voting shares.

Each successor requires a specific plan. Some may need to go back to school, others might work alongside a senior member to best learn how the business operates day-to-day, others yet may require a mentor or access to the Wisdom Council to guide them for the first year. For example, younger siblings in a family may not think that their older sister is ready to be the new CEO. Their concern can be diffused by assigning a respected board member with multiple industry perspectives as her mentor for the first year.

Adequate preparation requires a sufficient amount of time. This is one of the main reasons that succession planning needs to begin several years before the events take place. It provides the time to find a variety of candidates—family and non-family—and provide training and opportunities to grow into the role.

Creating a good ending to ownership

The very mention of the word "selling" can be a lightning bolt to some family members. Selling may sound like failure, even betrayal. The decision to keep or sell, however, is one of the issues that need to be faced during an open family conversation.

It should be made clear that the answer to "keep or sell?" is not mutually exclusive. Families can retain some ownership while protecting family wealth through a partial sale, or they can get out of the business side altogether and retain a successful enterprise by perhaps managing their own foundation (see chapter eight). Creating this kind of good ending to ownership is the secret for many families to preserve both their wealth and their family relationships.

Note that any discussion of buy or sell would include an assessment of the business from a long-term viability point of view. This is done separately from the family discussion in order to confirm that once the family interests are declared, the long-term plan supports the family's vision and values.

Final thoughts

The hit HBO series *Succession* portrays an aging patriarch of a media dynasty and his adult children who wrestle for control of the family company. In the first episode, the father suffers a debilitating stroke. This leaves his four children—none of whom have the ability to fill the job—scrambling to fill the power vacuum. Over a million viewers tune in to watch the drama and deceit that unfolds each week. The patriarch character loosely resembles Rupert Murdoch, whose sons James and Lachlan fought a nasty, decade-long battle over who would succeed their father.

No one wishes this kind of drama on their own family business!

It's the human side of the succession process that threatens to derail a family business from moving on to second and third generation ownership, not the legal, tax, or financial issues.

"Of course, I'll pass the business on to our children" is an assumption often in the mind of the parent/owner. In reality, however, the decision is rarely clear-cut. And even if it is, the same advice applies: it is in everyone's interest to integrate family members into the process early on, giving time for thoughtful discussion and for the practical issues around preparation.

If you haven't taken action yet, the preparation and planning needs to start now. You need about ten years to allow for the optimal development of an effective plan. That timeline also allows for the proper grooming of the successor.

By providing sufficient assurance to the current and future owners of the family business, and ensuring transparency to the family members every step of the way, succession planning can take place in a reasonable and open manner. The end result should then be what everyone wants: informed decisions on what is best for the business and for the family—with harmony preserved.

> "One of the things we often miss in succession planning is that it should be gradual and thoughtful, with lots of sharing of information and knowledge and perspective, so that it's almost a non-event when it happens."
>
> **ANNE M. MULCAHY** former CEO, Xerox

6

Let's Talk—The Family Meeting

Essential Conversations for Good Communication

In this chapter, we'll discuss:

- Topics every family business needs to talk about
- Elephants in the room
- Family meeting agendas and rules of conduct

FAMILY BUSINESS is clearly a mix of two worlds. We've talked a lot about having conversations around topics such as "What does the future look like in our business?" or "Who might be an obvious successor to groom for CEO?" It's important to acknowledge that these are not easy conversations. They are often referred to as "hard" or "difficult" conversations, or as addressing "the elephants in the room."

There are conversations that every family business needs to have that go beyond the day-to-day operations of the business. They are *essential* conversations because they are the glue that keeps the three circles connected, not just overlapping.

Below are six essential questions that every family business should consider asking at family meetings each year. There are some guiding notes after each question, but after that, you're on your own!

What does our family mean by wealth?

What kind of wealth do we have as a family? Are we rich?

What can we do to increase this wealth?

What can we do to share our wealth?

It's natural to think of wealth as "money," but family businesses measure their worth beyond just financial capital. Just listen to the stories at a family gathering about the obstacles overcome by the founders, or witness the family pride at a graduation celebration.

When answering this question, consider the following types of wealth:

- **People wealth:** those who have built the business and guided the family (family and non-family) in addition to the upcoming generation with their talents, enthusiasm, and new ideas.
- **Intellectual wealth:** the accumulated knowledge, experience, career achievements, etc. This includes that of those working in the business as well as those who have chosen a different career.
- **Spiritual wealth:** the belief that the family and the business are part of a greater whole with a larger purpose. This may be connected to religious faith, culture, or an appreciation of life's journey.

- **Social wealth:** the connection to the community outside the business activities through service and financial gifts.
- **Financial wealth:** financial capital makes everything else possible.

What is our approach to philanthropy?

What organizations do we want to support?

How do we want to implement our support?

How does our support align with our overall vision?

Philanthropy is acknowledged as a key element in keeping the bonds of a family strong across the generations. As high as eighty-one percent of the world's largest family businesses practice philanthropy (split between charitable donations and service to the community), and forty percent of family businesses have a family foundation.[15]

Giving money and volunteering talent are direct expressions of a family's core values. Philanthropic activity allows family members who aren't directly involved in the business to make meaningful contributions, perhaps by running or staffing a foundation or offering time as a volunteer.

Philanthropy also engages the younger generations of the family, helping them to make their own mark on the business and experience tangible examples of wealth beyond just the dollars.

How do we introduce the next generation to the business?

What does "working in the business" mean?

Is it something everyone is expected to do?

What can we do to make sure at least everyone has a choice?

How does someone "get" to work in the business?

Children are almost always involved in the business. Most helped out with countless tasks until they were old enough to have a summer job at the company. But when do you start talking to children about their future careers and what a job in the business means?

Various conditions can be drawn up once the family has had a healthy discussion on the topic. Some family businesses make it a rule that those who want a job in the business first have to complete post-secondary education. Others specify a length of time a young adult has to spend working in the business to gain experience (and to be evaluated) before they qualify to apply for a job.

What is family?

Who is "family" when we talk about the business?

What are the rights and privileges of in-laws?

Defining "family" is easy until you get past the first generation of ownership. Over time, others get added to the mix:

in-laws, stepchildren, stepparents, common-law partners, etc. Now expectations become blurred. One daughter-in-law is an excellent addition to the family business; the other is totally unsuited for any role at all. Do they both have a voice in family decisions? What about the owner who remarries? Your brother-in-law who brings his new wife to the decision-making table after he's divorced your sister?

How do we treat employees and owners who are not family members?

Do we have two "classes" of employees?

What can we do to make non-family members know they are included?

Non-family employees, perhaps a stellar CEO or a sales manager who is delivering spectacular results to a family firm, won't stick around if they constantly feel like "second-class citizens" compared to family members. Telling them they are part of the family business is not enough. Senior employees should be invited to at least part of the annual gathering and should be consulted when decisions that impact the business are being discussed. Many family firms hold separate company retreats in addition to the annual Family Assembly.

The same questions apply to non-family members who contribute as board members or shareholders. How do you demonstrate that their contribution is valued?

Does our vision align with our future?

What does the future look like? For individual members, for the founder, for the business?

How are we bringing our company vision and values to life?

The company vision statement and values (from chapter two) build trust and credibility by assuring family members that decisions are being made with purpose. Conversations about how a family business aligns its activities to its values need to be ongoing as the business evolves. What is changing? What needs to stay the same?

Elephants in the room

In addition to the essential conversations listed above, most family businesses face "elephant in the room" situations: conversations that no one wants to have but are critical, in many instances, for business viability and personal well-being. Some of the more common topics are substance and addiction problems, job performance and compensation, dishonesty or suspected illegal activities, physical/emotional abuse, anger management, and mental health.

Each of these call for an enormous amount of patience, empathy, tough love, and difficult decisions. They may be initially raised during a family meeting or a one-on-one interview. However, they are best dealt with by using an outside resource, such as an agency, facilitator, legal expert, or financial counsellor.

The value of the family meeting

Essential conversations need to happen in a trusted environment, where those in attendance know the purpose and agenda, and are provided guidelines (such as the rules of conduct) to ensure the time is spent effectively. As discussed earlier, the recommended forum is the annual Family Assembly or retreat, or smaller meetings such as the Family or Owners' Council. Some choose to talk about issues in break-out conversations at a larger meeting, and then come back and share with the group as a whole.

The agenda should be a mix of content and process, with time for breaks and activities.

- Content is the information sharing part, for example, updates from the owners on the financial health of the business or a review of the family vision.
- Process takes the form of questions that engage people in open discussion and encourage ideas. Questions should be open-ended so they can't be answered with an easy yes or no. Everyone should understand that the purpose is to hear everyone's voice, not make a final decision.
- Activities and extras are opportunities to hear family stories and history, outdoor/indoor games, celebrations, announcements and awards, and welcoming ice-breakers.

Setting the rules

It is recommended that the family members agree on how to engage with each other. In the bestselling business book *Crucial Conversations*, the authors suggest techniques for holding conversations in a "positive space" when surrounded by highly charged emotions. When applied to a family meeting, the rules could look something like this:

Each of us comes with an attitude of empathy and positive intentions because we believe that communication is the key to working and being better together.

As a family we commit:

- *To the mutual purpose to listen to and understand each other better, and to set a vision for guiding the business. (Or the purpose may be more specific: we commit to talking openly and honestly about succession.)*
- *To remain in dialogue—let's keep talking, even if we need to break into smaller groups*
- *To make it safe—no judging, no ridicule*
- *To keeping emotion under control—each of us can feel without our feelings clouding our reason*
- *To separate facts from story—we can learn from the past and the present to decide what we want for the future*
- *To agree to a clear action plan—we can trust others to make the final decisions after we've had our voices heard*

7

Emotional Intelligence and the Family Business

Nurturing skills and competencies for success and harmony

In this chapter, we'll discuss:

- The rise of emotional intelligence in business performance and leadership
- Emotional awareness as a skill set for navigating the complex waters of a family business
- The value of a growth mindset for family business

EMOTIONAL INTELLIGENCE is the ability to perceive and manage emotions in oneself and others; by doing so, we communicate better, work together better, and make more reasonable decisions by balancing facts with understanding.

In recent years, there's been an increasing amount of research into the positive influence of emotional intelligence on the family business.[16] The connection makes sense, especially when you look at the success factors required for a family business to beat the odds and move past the first, second, or even third generation of ownership. The qualities associated with a higher level of emotional intelligence—self-awareness, self-control, optimism, empathy, social awareness—are beneficial to all businesses but particularly to a family business, where the lines between personal and professional matters overlap.

The term "emotional intelligence" may be fairly new to you. It gained popularity in the mid-1990s when psychologist Daniel Goleman published his book on the subject. Since that time, emotional intelligence has been recognized for its correlation to success in work and personal life.

Educators, for example, encourage the development of emotional intelligence because it increases a student's ability to learn, be open to new ideas, and stay resilient in the face of challenges. Those working in leadership and organizational effectiveness encourage greater emotional intelligence because it enables collaboration and better communication, as well as helps individuals deal with conflict.

There are fifteen components associated with emotional intelligence. A selection follows, alongside examples of how those in a family business can encourage emotional intelligence as a way of keeping harmony and achieving greater business success.

Self-awareness

The ability to understand yourself clearly and objectively is a major factor when measuring emotional intelligence. Those who are self-aware recognize their own emotions and therefore are better able to keep their emotions in check when faced with difficult situations.

This is critical for the kinds of conversations bound to take place when parents, sons, daughters, siblings, cousins, and in-laws work together in a family business. The ability to perceive, understand, and acknowledge the way others feel in order to make them feel valued are critical factors in building harmony.

Perhaps there's a discussion about the future of the business and the founder's wish to retire. Someone with a quick temper could quickly derail options related to selling the business by shutting down the conversation with an angry response. However, with greater self-awareness, that same member could better manage their behaviour; they know that for them the topic of selling is a "hot button." The individual may still be upset but could at least say honestly to those around them, "I get angry when discussing this topic, but I understand that we do need to talk about it."

Self-regard or self-worth

Self-regard is the ability to accept and respect yourself. Those with self-regard understand their weaknesses and strengths, which makes them open to self-improvement. The internal motivation they feel means they are more likely to reach their potential. In turn, they are more willing to use their abilities to assist others to do the same.

You can see the power of this concept in a family business, particularly when it comes to hiring family members for positions such as CEO, or selecting the right candidates for board appointments.

Family enterprises need to find ways to offer as many opportunities as possible for family members to learn and experience the business. However, when it comes to assigning roles and responsibilities, decisions need to be based on merit, not emotion. This is the best way to achieve optimal business performance; it also creates good leaders and mentors. Promoting a family member because a parent feels "my son needs a chance" isn't good for business when that son fails. It certainly isn't good for the individual's sense of self-worth.

Many family businesses set up some kind of program whereby sons and daughter are given an opportunity to work in the business part-time while attending school. This not only gives the business an idea as to their suitability, it also gives the next generation an honest sense of what they're good at, what they need to learn, and where they might see themselves in the future.

Business families also have to be aware that some members may not feel included, which can feed resentment and lead to conflict down the road. Everyone needs to feel valued. Being encouraged to participate in the annual family meeting can be an effective way of motivating everyone to get involved. Some family foundations set up a discretionary spending budget that allows family members to finance projects that interest them. Others give them opportunities to serve on the board or staff of a foundation.

Assertiveness

It is easy to see why assertiveness (standing up for yourself) is essential, in particular in the Family Circle. There are always going to be family members who talk more than others or come across as the ones who know it all. Plus, the dynamics of birth order are always at play. The youngest likely won't have the same experience or level of involvement in the business as the eldest. There also may be perceived favourites in a family, such as the daughter who works alongside her father every day.

Every family member needs to be able to have their voice heard, while respecting the experience and knowledge of others. Such assertiveness helps prevent conflict because feelings and interests are aired in a "safe space," instead of being ignored or repressed. This can be very valuable when topics come up such as sibling rivalry, favouritism (real or imagined), or unreasonable expectations.

Family meetings with the purpose of gaining input, knowledge, and understanding from everyone are a positive way to encourage such assertiveness. A family member may not agree with the discussion that's taking place, but ideally a conversation at a family meeting provides a forum for honest reflection and multiple viewpoints.

Independence

Independence is another component that can get overlooked in a family business but is critical for maintaining positive self-image and assertiveness. So much in a family business is about "what's best for the business." Those who don't want to participate as fully as others may feel like they are letting the family down. They may even suffer repercussions from a parent who's deeply disappointed with their disinterest in the company.

Not everyone in a family business, however, may want a role. Perhaps they want to set up their own business or work outside the company while retaining an ownership interest. This can be a very difficult revelation to a parent-founder who's dreamed all their life that one day their child would step into their shoes.

There are various ways to foster independence. A family business is ideally suited to give those in the upcoming generation the hands-on experience and knowledge they need in order to make a decision about their future. Some family businesses even make it a rule that everyone works at least a few years in the business before making the decision to stay or pursue another career. After this time, if a son or daughter decides to set up their own business or go into a profession such as law, everyone can be satisfied that it was an informed decision.

With this kind of process in place, family members who choose a different path are able to assert their independence but remain connected and, in many instances, an essential part of the enterprise—but from outside the firm. Instead of assuming that a daughter or son take on a particular role, that son or daughter can speak with confidence about their own vision and goals and in turn be supported and encouraged in their decisions.

Empathy

Empathy is the ability to understand other people's feelings, emotions, and desires. People with little empathy do not recognize their own emotions. They assign blame to others and avoid taking responsibility, instead of trying to find a solution that works for everyone. On the other hand, people with empathy are able to put themselves in the situations of others and recognize what is driving their behaviour. Those around them feel understood. Empathetic people tend to be better at negotiating and making decisions that others support.

There are many instances in all three circles of the family business where empathy is invaluable. Empathy helps parents better understand what their adult children want, even when it differs from their own wants. Empathy helps siblings and extended family members better understand the vision of the owner and their passion and drive to make the business succeed.

Associated with empathy is the ability to be realistic and flexible. Conflict resolution, in particular, calls on the ability to empathize, be realistic, and exercise flexibility. Those who are realistic don't pretend that something isn't happening. They know what is going on and face it with a practical attitude. Individuals who are flexible are open to new ideas, new ways for doing things, and new circumstances—whether they welcome them or not.

There are many examples in a family business where the above skills need to be encouraged and supported.

For instance, it is never going to be easy dealing with the issues that arise in a blended family. Let's say a beloved mother dies, and the father remarries. The children not only have to deal with someone taking the place of their mother, they also have to cope with someone outside the family involved in decision-making. It is only by listening to each other, drawing on empathy and making an effort to be flexible and realistic that families get through such challenges.

The same applies when families face difficult conversations around substance abuse, for example. No one is being asked to agree that this is acceptable behaviour, but they do need to accept that the problem exists—that is, be realistic about it. They also need to admit that the path forward is not going to be easy and seek professional help. All of this takes empathy, flexibility, and a high dose of realism.

Putting oneself in another's shoes is an excellent way to build trust and communication. Empathy is such an important concept that families may choose to highlight it as one of their guiding principles for family meetings.

Stress tolerance and self-control

Clearly, stress tolerance is required in a family business, particularly in those areas where the three circles overlap. The failure of a business to meet financial goals creates tremendous pressure on management. Management's failure to live up to its potential puts pressure on the owners. The impact from family members facing personal crises, such as divorce or illness, ripples across all areas of the business. Even good changes, such as a marriage or change in ownership, bring a level of stress.

Leaders and managers who have developed stress tolerance possess the emotional intelligence attribute of self-control. Self-control makes it possible for them to focus on a long-term goal when a lightning bolt hits, rather than react unthinkingly under pressure. They also are ready to act calmly when they see an opportunity.

No one wants the worst-case scenario where a sibling is fired by their father after a heated personal argument. But there are going to be times when it's necessary to make a difficult decision about management. Perhaps it is time to hire a new CEO, which means removing a family member who is not performing to expectations.

Having policies and rules in place related to HR issues, such as performance and bonus payments, is an excellent way to support stress tolerance in a family business. By taking emotion out of the Business Circle, those facing difficult choices are better able to apply reasonable thought in order to keep decisions strategic, not personal.

Social responsibility

It's no surprise that concern for the greater good is part of emotional intelligence. A sense of social responsibility dovetails perfectly with the corresponding values that keep family businesses strong and united.

There are many ways that a family can encourage social responsibility, particularly for the next generation. All ages can take time at family gatherings to reflect on what philanthropy has meant to them through the years. Conversations about succession planning can include topics such as "What is family wealth?" and "What do we want as our legacy?"

Those new to the company as well as family members at all stages of life can benefit from direct experience working with a charity supported by the business. Most not-for-profit organizations offer onsite visits or opportunities to work on a project (e.g., Habitat for Humanity). These kinds of activities are extremely beneficial in building social responsibility as well as bringing the family together to improve relationships and communication.

Optimism

Those with high emotional intelligence view obstacles as challenges. Nowhere is this kind of optimism more apparent than in a family business. Built right into the entrepreneurial spirit that founded a company is the belief in all possibilities. Such passion was certainly at work during the COVID-19 crisis when many struggling family businesses found new ways to make income through online sales or to add value in a meaningful way. For example, a Toronto custom tailor business switched to making bespoke face masks. Dillon's Distillery in Beamsville, Ontario, turned from gin manufacture to hand sanitizer and disinfectant production.

A family business can encourage optimism by taking every opportunity to remember and celebrate the founder's vision. This is why it's wise to begin annual family meetings by telling stories together about the history and celebrating the past year's accomplishments beyond just financial successes. These activities reinforce a sense of pride, a positive attitude, and an enduring belief that the family can overcome whatever challenges come their way.

Putting it all together

The above is just a sampling of what emotional intelligence can teach a family business. The resulting growth mindset that comes with a higher level of emotional intelligence is a critical factor in directing a family business toward greater opportunities and in turn greater financial success.

As we've read, many of these skills are already at play in the three circles of business, family, and ownership; others can be developed and supported through the various process and systems covered in this book.

- Family rules and family governance systems provide a way to manage emotions in order to hear, understand, and accept facts and alternate viewpoints.
- A family constitution and values statement identify (and distinguish between) personal and business concerns.
- Family meetings are an ideal forum for building trust: decisions that have to be made for the business can be done with everyone satisfied that their voice has been heard.

The summary below charts the categories covered by emotional intelligence skills. Ask yourself, "How strong are my own emotional intelligence skills? What could be done to help improve my skills and those of the members of our family business?"

Self-perception

Do you respect yourself and accept your strengths and weaknesses?

Are you always willing to try to improve yourself and engage in activities that lead to a more enjoyable life?

Do you recognize and understand your emotions?

Do you understand the cause of your emotions and the impact they have on your thoughts and actions, and how they affect others?

Self-expression

What are the ways that you express emotions (verbally and non-verbally)?

Are you able to communicate your feelings, beliefs, and thoughts openly and defend your rights and values in a socially acceptable way?

Are you free from emotional dependency on others? That is, can you accept how you feel without blaming someone else? Are you able to make your own decisions and then take responsibility for carrying out your own plan?

Interpersonal relationships

How good are you at developing relationships that are mutually satisfying and characterized by trust and compassion?

Do you recognize, understand, and appreciate how other people feel? Can you support them in a way that respects the person's feelings, even when you don't agree with what they are doing?

Decision-making

Can you solve problems when there are emotions involved? Can you stick with it?

Do you understand how emotions affect decision-making?

Can you stay objective and see things as they really are? Do you think clearly and see both sides?

Can you delay or resist impulses, decisions, or rash choices? Are you stopping to think?

Stress management

Can you adapt emotions, thoughts, and behaviours to unfamiliar, unpredictable circumstances or ideas?

Can you cope with stressful or difficult situations? Do you believe that you can manage or influence situations in a positive way?

Do you have a positive attitude on life? Do you tend to stay hopeful and resilient?

8

The Rise of the Family Enterprise

Moving from Wealth to Legacy

In this chapter, we'll discuss:

- The Family Office
- The rise of the family enterprise
- Moving forward with confidence

SEVERAL YEARS AGO, our team worked with a family that made the decision to get out of the family business. They sold the company, but instead of dividing out the money, they put the bulk of it into a holding company, which they agreed to manage together. Then they invested in an investment portfolio and several real estate properties.

Although they were no longer an operating business, they remained an active, vital family enterprise that worked together, planned together, and made a difference in the world around them together. They continued to hold family meetings with an annual retreat to keep the lines of communication open and make sure everyone felt included. They also continued to monitor their vision and goals; one of which was to find ways to instill the entrepreneurial spirit in the next generation. As a result, they set up a foundation with a scholarship fund. Past owners and the founder are part of the program, which includes mentoring young adults in the family wishing to pursue a career in business.

The family is truly a thriving enterprise, with a mission statement that aligns with the values established years ago when the founder first opened the business.

Many families are surprised to hear a family enterprise described in this way. They've only thought of being in business or *not* being in business. Selling the family firm and transitioning to an ongoing enterprise can be equally special and rewarding, both financially and in terms of harmony and fulfilment. Instead of being the "end," the sale (and its proceeds) brings family members together who want to pursue common interests, often with the addition of a foundation to support charity and continuing education.

The Family Office

When a family enterprise is no longer connected with an operating business, there still is a need for professional resources, such as legal counsel, investment and tax services, estate planning, and so on. A recent entrant into the professional services market that provides such support is a variation on a traditional Family Office.

In the simplest explanation, a Family Office is a formal structure set up by a family to manage its wealth and everything that goes with it. The concept is modelled after large, complex, single family offices associated with high-wealth families, particularly in the US. In these instances, however, the office includes actual buildings with staff who manage the family's wealth, foundations, and personal lives. The Rockefeller Family Office, for instance, has been managing billions of US dollars and assets on behalf of the family, its businesses, and philanthropic interests since

1882. In Canada, there are the Thompson Family and the Weston Family Offices, among others.

Most family businesses don't fall into the above category. However, a variation of the Family Office is now offered through the private wealth management services of banks and consulting firms. A Family Office, such as CIBC Family Office, offers pooled resources and expertise in personal financial management, business succession and legacy planning, investment management, and fiduciary services. Families that take advantage of these services may be operating a business or, as discussed above, have transitioned to a different kind of family enterprise.

Using the resources of a Family Office can be an excellent way to support the ongoing enterprise. The family, through the Family Council, remains the unit that gives families a chance to bond, teach young members how to be knowledgeable shareholders, and to vote (or have their voices heard). When required, the Family Office may also provide support in areas such as facilitation, counselling, conflict resolution, planning, and managing.

The future is yours, and it's bright

A friend of mine is president of a family-owned company, although he is not a family member. Like businesses around the world during the COVID-19 pandemic, the company faced financial challenges when non-essential services were ordered to shut down. With demand for their goods at a stand-still, one of the big questions at the company became "How do we pay our bills, in particular, our staff salaries?"

My friend suggested that the shareholders, a father and his adult children, voluntarily scale back the dividends they receive for a few months—after all, the money was just a bonus for them.

The reaction was disappointing. Instead of thinking about the plight of the staff, the overall health of the company, and the shared crisis that literally impacted economies around the world, family shareholders could only think about their own paycheques and how they'd be so hard done by with such a decision.

For those of us who've studied and worked with family businesses over the years, this kind of reaction is an indicator of the overall future of the firm. When owners or leaders in a family business put themselves and their personal interests before the greater good of the enterprise, it almost inevitably spells its ultimate demise.

This is, perhaps, the greatest lesson to be learned for a family business. In the end, it's not the business you are protecting, nurturing, and growing; it is the enterprise. And the enterprise is so much more than just the daily operations of a factory, a chain of restaurants, or a construction company.

This is, perhaps, the greatest lesson to be learned for a family business. In the end, it's not the business you are protecting, nurturing, and growing; it is the enterprise. And the enterprise is so much more than just the daily operations of a factory, a chain of restaurants, or a construction company.

A family business provides the means for building wealth and directing complete wealth wisely in business, investing, living, and giving. Family businesses that survive find ways to maintain a balance between business goals (growth, innovation, recruiting talented staff) and family goals (maintaining family values, protecting family wealth). They also plan for a smooth transition in leadership and ownership from one generation to the next.

The Three Circle Model helps separate the three overlapping interests. This is a constant reminder of what makes a family business both unique and challenging. The various interests and resulting goals are going to be different; it's how you communicate with each other and work through the conflict that makes the difference.

You now have some practical ways and governance recommendations to help.

- By using the various systems described in this book, e.g., family meetings and a constitution, your business will have the means to communicate and live out its values internally and externally.

- By having a strong sense of vision beyond yourself, you will survive from generation to generation and continue to foster a sense of pride in the company's contribution to society.
- By developing and acting on your values and vision with full involvement from family members, you will always be able to identify a purpose that's larger than a single business or personal interest.
- By preparing for the lightning bolts, you will be ready when change comes—and you will get through it.
- By using various tools, such as questions to ask during "essential conversations," you will continue to build trust and transparency and open doors for new business partners and opportunities, including (when the time comes) succession planning.
- By using resources such as emotional intelligence skills, you will discover that you have more in common with each other than you may think, including strong shared ethical standards and common goals. This will strengthen family cohesion and help you make better decisions.
- By continuing to meet, talk, develop, and interpret your governance systems, constitution, and rules of conduct through family meetings over the generations, you will

have the resources in place to keep the enterprise moving forward.

All of this will give your most precious resource—your family—continued pride in what you have achieved and a clear way for ensuring harmony and prosperity for current and future generations.

Best wishes to each of you!

Notes

1. *Family Enterprise Matters: Harnessing the Most Powerful Driver of Economic Growth in Canada* (Family Enterprise Xchange Foundation, 2019), https://family-enterprise-xchange.com/resource/family-enterprise-matters.
2. *In Harmony: Family Business Cohesion and Profitability* (EY and Kennesaw State University's Cox Family Enterprise Center, 2017).
3. Roy Williams and Vic Preisser, *Preparing Heirs: Five Steps to a Successful Transition of Family Wealth and Values* (The Williams Group, 2003).
4. Grant Walsh, *Family Business Succession: Managing the All-Important Family Component* (KPMG, 2011).
5. *A Primer on Governance of the Family Enterprise* (The Wharton School of the University of Pennsylvania and the Leonard N. Stern School of Business of New York University, World Economic Forum, June 2013).
6. For more on Patricia Angus, see https://angusadvisorygroup.com.
7. The five values were adapted in 2010 after a comprehensive consultation with different stakeholders. These values are displayed Henkel's headquarters in Düsseldorf.
8. *Global Family Business Survey 2018* (PwC, 2018), https://www.pwc.com/gx/en/services/family-business/family-business-survey-2018.html.
9. Alistair MacDonald, "In Canada, a Feud Divides the Irving Family Empire," *WSJ*, August 4, 2014, https://www.wsj.com/

articles/in-canada-a-feud-divides-the-irving-family-empire-1407205802.
10. John Lorinc, "Don't Let Your Family Destroy Your Business," *Canadian Business*, January 22, 2015, https://www.canadianbusiness.com/innovation/dont-let-your-family-destroy-your-business.
11. "The Disintegration of the Irving Family," book excerpt, *The Globe and Mail*, November 2, 2014, https://www.theglobeandmail.com/report-on-business/the-disintegration-of-the-irving-family/article21420018.
12. Kimberly Eddleston, "The 'Fredo Factor': How Deadbeats and Troublemakers Hurt Family Business," FamilyBusiness.org, June 13, 2017, https://familybusiness.org/content/the-fredo-factor-how-deadbeats-and-troublemakers.
13. Bill and Melinda Gates, "We Didn't See This Coming," Gates Notes, February 12, 2019, https://www.gatesnotes.com/2019-Annual-Letter.
14. *Once in a Lifetime: Moving Canadian Private and Family Businesses Forward* (PwC), https://www.pwc.com/ca/en/private-company-services/assets/pwc-canada-once-in-a-lifetime-report.pdf.
15. *Family Business Philanthropy: Creating Lasting Impact Through Values and Legacy* (EY Family Business Center of Excellence, 2016), https://familybusiness.ey-vx.com/pdfs/1003645-family-business-philanthropy-lr.pdf.
16. For a sample of the research into this area, see https://scholar.google.ca/scholar?q=emotional+intelligence+and+family+business&hl=en&as_sdt=0&as_vis=1&oi=scholart.

About the author

Fred Guzzi, CFA, CFP, CIM, FEA, FMA, FCSI
Senior Wealth Advisor, Senior Portfolio Manager

ALBANO MARTINS PHOTOGRAPHY

FRED GUZZI is a highly respected Senior Wealth Advisor and Senior Portfolio Manager at CIBC Wood Gundy, CIBC Private Wealth, a premier provider of wealth management services in Canada. Whether he is advising a family business or providing consulting advice to a charitable organization, Fred always brings his strong work ethic and an unwavering commitment to meeting the investment needs of his clients.

As the son of hard-working immigrant parents, Fred learned that a strong work ethic and drive to succeed could build wealth. He also came to understand the importance of customized, trusted advice to help families reach their financial goals and achieve family harmony.

Fred joined CIBC Wood Gundy as an Investment Advisor shortly after graduating from the University of Toronto. When CIBC Private Wealth set up its first Family Enterprise Office, Fred was named as one of a few leading advisors across the country to set up his own group in this specialty area of wealth management. Since then, the Guzzi Wealth Management Group has worked with business owners, professionals, affluent families, foundations, charitable organizations, and associations to help them achieve their goals and build long-term sustainability.

In addition to his designation as an FEA (Family Enterprise Advisor), Fred's certifications include CFA (Chartered Financial Analyst), CFP (Certified Financial Planner), CIM (Canadian Investment Manager), FMA (Financial Management Advisor), and FCSI (Fellow of CSI, Certified Securities Institute)—the highest financial services credential in the Canadian financial services industry.

The significance of the entrepreneurial spirit, family cohesion, and community outreach are central to how Fred lives his daily life. When he's not spending time with family, it's not unusual to find Fred putting together backpacks and survival kits for the homeless or participating in various charities supported by CIBC, such as CIBC Children's Miracle Day.

Fred lives in Toronto with his wife and two children.

Made in United States
Cleveland, OH
05 November 2026

47664322R00080